CLIFF

A CELEBRATION

Photographs by

Theresa Wassif

Bill Latham, part of Cliff's management team and a close personal friend, has written the text and the all-important captions, which complement the photographs and add interesting insights into Cliff's career and life.

Theresa Wassif, a freelance photographer, followed Cliff around the world for over a year to take the stunning original shots featured in this unique photographic collection.

Dear Gillian – A little pressie for you to add to your
"Cliff" collection. Lots & lots of love,
Mommy & Daddy.
September, 1991.
xxx

CLIFF
A CELEBRATION

Photographs by

Theresa Wassif

HODDER AND STOUGHTON
LONDON SYDNEY AUCKLAND TORONTO

Acknowledgements and Thanks

ELINCHROM – for their support in providing lighting equipment.

All thanks, praise and glory to God.

British Library Cataloguing in Publication Data
Wassif, Theresa
  Cliff: a celebration.
  1. Pop music. Singing. Richard, Cliff – Biographies
  I. Title   II. Latham, Bill
  784.5′0092′4

ISBN 0-340-50273 8   Pbk
ISBN 0-340-50269 X   Hb

First published in Great Britain 1989.
Second impression 1989

Published by Hodder and Stoughton,
a division of Hodder and Stoughton Ltd,
Mill Road, Dunton Green, Sevenoaks, Kent TN13 2YA
Editorial Office: 47 Bedford Square, London WC1B 3DP

Designed by Design & Art

Photoset by Rowland Phototypesetting Ltd, Bury St Edmunds, Suffolk.

Printed in Great Britain by Butler & Tanner Ltd, Frome and London.

CONTENTS

INTRODUCTION

I guess it's another first – for me, at least! There have been books a-plenty telling the Cliff story in words – and I've contributed a few of those myself – but it's the first time, as far as I know, that anyone's tried to depict my life via a collection of photographs. Somehow I feel they're just as eloquent, if not more so.

All credit to Theresa Wassif for tackling the task. Theresa is a young photographer who came to my attention a few years ago with some really good stage and studio shots. For me the very basic test of any photographer is, 'Does he or she make me look good?' That's becoming an increasingly difficult challenge as the years go by! The camera, they say, never lies. In the words of the politician, however, I'm happy for it to be 'economical with the truth'!

For a year, Theresa seemed to be dogging my footsteps. She followed us on tour in Australia and Europe. She popped up in theatres, studios and churches, and crept into interviews, meetings and recording sessions. Somehow she got me to agree to letting her take pictures at home. Even the dog seemed co-operative, if not exactly enthusiastic! A similar response, I imagine, to some of my camera-shy management team who, I see, have a page or two to themselves. . . !

Apparently this is a 'coffee-table book'. Whether that's a euphemism for 'downright expensive', I don't know! If your coffee-table is anything like mine, it would soon be submerged under the clutter of halfeaten boxes of chocolates, TV magazines, remote control

gadgets, umpteen videos and cassettes, and associated junk waiting to be tidied up. *If* it's all the same to you, *I*'ll keep my copy where *I* can find it!

This, by the way, is *Theresa*'s very first book, and personally *I*'m proud to have been the subject of all her subtle and discreet focus. *I* hope the book does well for her and that you, the reader – or is it viewer? – will enjoy the glimpse into my privileged world.

Cliff

HOME

. . . they say, is where the heart is. Perhaps that isn't strictly true in Cliff's case, but it is certainly where he finds peace and much pleasure. Few of us can imagine what it must be like to lose all semblance of anonymity outside our front door. Instant recognition may have its advantages in some situations, but it can be a gnawing pressure when even a visit to the Chinese take-away means being gawped at, sized up and publicly 'on display'. Home is where Cliff can look sloppy and unshaven, and no one will mutter snide abuse or grab an arm for autographs. Home is where Emma, the pet Westie, will smile a welcome, and where the armchair is somehow more comfortable than those at the most exclusive hotel. The house is grand by any standard, but don't expect rare art treasures, silver collections, or precious antiques. Visitors say it's a comfortable home – relaxed and warm-feeling – but if houses reflect the people who inhabit them, that's hardly surprising.

Emma, the West Highland terrier, was a gift
from the fan club. She's no Crufts medallist but
has been faithful companion, squirrel-chaser,
and head of security for eleven years. Rumour
has it that she sleeps in Cliff's bedroom!

The telephone for Cliff is like a mail delivery
– it's best ignored!

Kitchen gadgetry poses no great problem
for the man who once claimed he'd relish the
job of a restaurant waiter. Cliff is happy to
cook for three or four; any larger number gets
him flummoxed. His speciality is gravy!

One of the rare 'through the keyhole' glimpses
into the home Cliff so obviously enjoys and
takes a pride in.

There are few refusals when Cliff throws a
party. This group of friends, mainly
management and band members, gathered for
a retirement celebration for long-term
colleague, Ron King.

Cliff's home and garden are the perfect
setting for a summer party. The long patio
overlooking sweeping lawns, colourful flower
beds, a fifty-foot pool and luxury pool house,
are an estate agent's dream.

NINETEEN

XIX 58 ⇨

PEOPLE

The applause said it all. When Cliff announced from the stage at Brighton that 'Mistletoe and Wine' had made it to Number One, the reaction was remarkable. 'It wasn't just polite applause to congratulate me,' said Cliff. 'It was as if they were personally sharing and feeling my success. They couldn't have been more ecstatic if they'd recorded the song themselves.'

That seems to be the hallmark of people in the Cliff Richard orbit. Fans, management, band, writers, producers – all of them regard Cliff as more than a hobby, an employer or a sideline. Somehow he inspires extraordinary loyalty, and it's the reason why the faces around the man have changed little – except to get older – over the years. Lasting relationships aren't exactly commonplace in the fickle world of showbusiness: expediency often determines who does what for whom. Yet somehow you get the feeling that an awful lot of people would give their right arm rather than let Cliff down. A great army of fans has followed his every move over the decades.

Peter Gormley Management, now evolved into the Cliff Richard Organisation, has been effectively 'doing the business' almost since Day One. And EMI have been understandably delighted to renew contracts ever since 'Move It' first coined them a quid or two in the late '50s.

It cannot be mere good fortune that has led to this sort of stability and consistent back-up. Maybe it's simply a matter of 'birds of a feather' . . . Whatever the reason, the power, or powers, aren't so much behind the throne in Cliff's case, but right alongside it, and it's a formidable force.

David Bryce

David has been associated with Cliff's career virtually since it began, and the distinctive hairstyle has become almost a trademark of the Cliff Richard retinue! After Peter Gormley's retirement in the mid-1980s, David took over the reins as professional manager, and his experience and practical know-how within the music industry result in unique and priceless input.

Malcolm Smith

From management offices in Esher, Surrey, Malcolm directs all of Cliff's financial and business affairs. He is in over-all charge of the Cliff Richard Organisation – the umbrella title for the whole gamut of Cliff's business and professional activities.

Bill Latham

With David and Malcolm, Bill is the third member of the management trio. Since the mid-1960s, he has steered Cliff's Christian and charity involvements and has principally looked after what could be loosely described as the non-commercial diary. As director of Cliff's Charitable Trust, he deals with the deluge of charitable requests that pours into the office each day and, more recently, has taken responsibility for all press and media coverage.

Peter Gormley

Photographs of Peter Gormley are few but, if anyone should share the credit for Cliff's remarkable career, it's this camera-shy, hugely-respected Australian. From 1960 to his retirement in the mid-1980s, Peter was Cliff's manager and built a reputation for straight dealing, honesty, and tough negotiation that was second to none in the music industry. His loyalty to Cliff was, and still is, unswerving and his wise counsel invaluable. Many of the older generation in the business will always think of Cliff simply as 'Peter Gormley's boy'. And that says it all.

Gill Snow

There would be no shortage of takers for Gill Snow's job. As Cliff's
secretary, Gill deals with the massive daily postbag which arrives
at the management office and at Cliff's house, and is the voice at the
other end of the line to scores of callers wanting information,
advice or simply Cliff himself!

Ron King

Ron King was a hard act to follow. As Cliff's tour PA, driver and right-hand-man for more years than anyone cares to remember, he was well-nigh irreplaceable. For Ron nothing was ever too much trouble, no crisis ever too big to handle. An incorrigible backstage wind-up merchant, he was the teller of endless showbiz anecdotes which could and should fill a book. After the 1988 Australian tour, Ron retired, wanting to be more permanently at home with his wife. He needed more time, he said, to 'smell the roses'.

Roger Bruce

The role of Cliff's PA on tour demands a rare versatility. From organising appointments and stage clothes to dealing with fans and theatre management, the job is tailor-made for a practically-minded diplomat who is a stickler for detail and a barrel of laughs. Meet Roger.

Bob Hellyer

Virtually every concert review in recent years has heaped praise on the remarkable light show which has been an integral part of a Cliff concert. Much of the credit for the striking and creative effects is due to lighting designer and operator Bob Hellyer. Watching him at work at the control desk is in itself an experience, and Bob is another of the technical crew who invariably is on 'top priority' standby.

John Seymour

Production manager, set designer, and general handyman, John Seymour is one of those practical do-it-yourself guys which no self-respecting office should be without. Another team member whose years of association run into double figures.

Colin Norfield

It is vital for any artist to have one hundred per cent confidence in the man who operates the sound desk. He has the power to make a vocal sound rich and clear or shrill and distorted. For Cliff, Colin Norfield is No 1 choice every time. Each hall has its acoustic peculiarities and requires its own precise sound settings and levels. Each instrument and backing vocal needs to be mixed and balanced to achieve the desired over-all effect. Today, sound amplification is a science, and Colin is a master of it.

John James

As monitor engineer and technical 'boffin', JJ is the other half of Cliff's sound team. It's as crucial for the artist and musicians on stage to hear clean uncluttered sound as it is for the audience. With half a dozen other instruments belting out their music only a yard or so away from their ears, it is imperative that each musician hears his own contribution among the cacophony. Operating the desk at the side of the stage, it's JJ who is in the firing line for hisses and frantic signals if levels and balance aren't spot on.

The proudest of mums and sisters. Cliff's family
has remained closely united over the years, and
the current tally of nieces and nephews is ten!
Pictured here, left to right, are: Joan; Donna;
and Cliff's mum, Dorothy. Jacqui is the missing
third sister.

NINETEEN

XIX 64 ⟡

TOURING

Rehearsals in some cramped studio or soulless warehouse signal the end of things normal – like walking the dog, deadheading the roses, or marinading the steaks. They herald a changed lifestyle, strange beds, and a new, sometimes manic, family.

Cliff has lost count of how many times he has fronted a tour, but barely a year of the last thirty has gone by without at least one. Since 1958 it's reckoned that he has spent on average three months a year 'on the road'. No wonder there's a sort of routine.

During rehearsals, stage clothes are brought in for storage in the tour wardrobe – that's easy. Cliff knows what he wants, and buys his outfits well in advance. Personal packing is last-minute and invariably a panic. Three a.m. and there's still indecision. Changes of climate and vastly different situations require everything from sloppy casual to smart formal. Always he packs too much, yet somehow crams it all into two cases. More recently he's added a sports bag and racquet case, which give him more the appearance of a tennis pro. Then there's the Walkman and tapes, speakers for hotel rooms, vitamin pills, and those indispensable, almost threadbare, comedy cassettes to lull him to sleep. If there's room, squeeze in the camera, and check once more for the passport.

In the morning it's a drag saying goodbye, and the dog knows she's due for another long stint of window-watching. The tail droops pathetically and it's better not to look.

At the airport, partings are done, and the mood is up. Band and engineers are already into their various comedy routines, and management are doing their best to manage. Few spare a thought for the drivers of the massive pantechnicons which trundled away thirty-six hours before, with twenty-five tons of lighting rig, sound equipment and stage set.

Everything suddenly slides into automatic. Check in at the hotel, suss out the rooms, the sauna and the health club. For Cliff it's predictable and routinely under control. The bed board is under the mattress, as requested; flowers are by courtesy of EMI. Champagne is on ice, with compliments of the house manager; no one has told him Cliff prefers pink! Usually the suite is comfortable, even luxurious. Sometimes Cliff swaps it for a regular room if early morning traffic noise is tiresome. Even a broom cupboard is better, if it means an uninterrupted night's sleep.

Five minutes after arrival there's an informal meeting in the office – better known to other guests as the hotel coffee shop. Social agendas are planned, and the combined wisdom of the more seasoned is applied to eating out. Indian, Chinese, Mexican – the Gourmet Club are sure to know the pick of what's on offer.

But first there's the concert. Sound check at 5 p.m. Somehow it's always a relief to spot the trucks already parked up. The 'get-in' has been done and most things are ready – all too often after some hassle, and even frayed tempers. Crew work is demanding and backbreaking at the best of times and, as the tour progresses, it's no surprise to find this special breed of sinewy masochists flaked out on top of flight cases or wherever, oblivious to backstage pandemonium and blaring decibels. It could be their only sleep for twenty-four hours.

For Cliff, the dressing-room is the only oasis for the coming hours. Often it's small, sparsely furnished, and badly lit. Putting on make-up, particularly around the eyes, can be a hazardous guessing game. The thoughtful crew will have anticipated the problem, and temporary lights will already be rigged. It seems impossible that anyone on the touring team – around twenty-five in all – could overlook the smallest responsibility. Everything is professional and finely tuned. Cliff selects stage clothes from the wardrobe, and it's left to his personal assistant to iron and ensure that everything is exactly as required. A missing sock or a broken shoelace could be time-wasting disasters!

Pre-concert sound balancing is critical. Every hall and arena has its own peculiar acoustics, and the man at the controls has to get it exactly right. Vocals and instruments must sound 'just like the record', and that takes skill and a good ear. Cliff's own 'warm-up' may take half an hour, sometimes longer. For venue staff, preparing for the audience invasion, it's a bonus. Cliff alone at the mike, with just an acoustic guitar, running through classic ad lib rock 'n' roll. Last-minute adjustments go on around him with minimum fuss. Lights are properly focused, musicians tinker with amps, ramps and risers are checked for safety. The voice is in good shape. The stage is set. The magic is ready to be switched on. Within minutes the public are swarming for their seats, and the chatter almost drowns the taped music.

The dressing-room, by comparison, is tranquil – virtually a no-go area, except for the authorised. Make-up now accentuates the eyes and jawline. Jeans and T-shirt are exchanged for sharp, loose-fitting jacket and trousers. Matching trainers complete the outfit. Next door, the band are still matching pun for pun. Musicians' humour is in a class of its own. Five minutes before show-time Cliff joins the band and, on the first night at least, conversation might turn to music. If anyone has nerves, no one would guess!

In the wings, technicians are involved in a last-minute scramble. There is always something not quite right, but it's seldom serious. Three minutes after eight, and the concert's underway. Cliff's not an artist to keep his audience waiting.

During intermission, a pile of flowers, chocolates and toys is brought from the stage to the dressing-room. Cliff has little opportunity to take notice. Drying off, a few minutes resting flat out on the floor, a change of clothes, and a check on the hair is all there's time for. No one, but no one, is invited to the dressing-room during intermission.

The second half shoots by. Cliff can't believe he's taking his bow for the last number.

Again, everything is waiting in the dressing-room. A hot towel, and a glass of cheap champagne and pineapple juice are priorities. It used to be port and honey, but tastes change. Now there are enough flowers and gifts to start a shop. A local hospital or children's home will be grateful.

Within minutes, sound and lighting men are round, asking if all was well. It's much more than a formality. All part of the fine-tuning and, if anything's wrong, it will be right next time. The pile of wet, sweaty clothes is dumped in a plastic bag for immediate attention, and Cliff's back in familiar everyday gear. A brief inquest on the show with management, and it's time to wheel in the visitors. Local dignitaries and DJs, record company men, competition winners, and always a batch of autographs for each one – 'And just one more, please, for my sister'! It's not Cliff's favourite pastime, especially after a two-and-a-half hour physical work-out, but he's patient and goes on smiling.

Finally, there's the stage door, and that can be a battle. The Gourmet Club are waiting, and he won't have eaten since toast and honey that morning. If there's a genuine rush, he'll leave by a side exit, but most times he plays the game and meets the fans. After more autographs and endless flash photographs, he makes the car, and the work's done.

The meal is great, in bed by 2, up at 11, tennis at 1. And that's how it is for six weeks. Even as talk and thoughts turn more towards home, morale seldom flags, and the last concert is as tight and as important as the first.

'. . . a new and sometimes manic family!'

Farewell, England – yet again.

Maybe the reason why concert tickets cost an
arm and a leg.

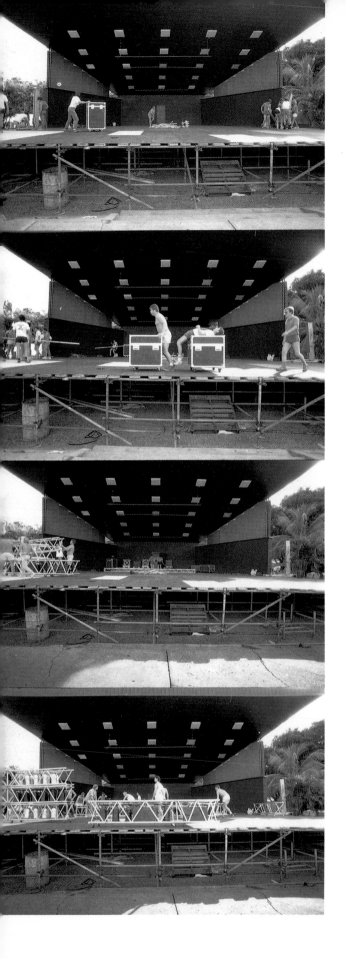

Something from nothing.

Hotels are largely what you make them!

Just be thankful it doesn't bite!

In the '60s they said he was finished.

More stage magic.

NINETEEN

XIX 70 ⮕

Ayers Rock in the eye of the beholder.

aUSTRaLIa

ANSETT AIRLINES FLIGHT DEPART 9.45am ARRIVE

ANSETT AIRLINES FLIGHT DEPART 7.00am ARRIVE

QANTAS DEPART 5.45pm

ANSETT AIRLINES FLIGHT DEPART 8.40am ARRIVE

ANSETT AIRLINES FLIGHT DEPART 12.00nn ARRIVE

ANSETT AIRLINES FLIGHT DEPART 8.25am ARRIVE

ANSETT AIRLINES FLIGHT DEPART 1.35pm ARRIVE

ADELAIDE TO BRISBANE WEDNESDAY 24 FEBRUARY

ANSETT AIRLINES DEPART 11.00am

COOLANGATTA TO SYDNEY

ANSETT AIRLINES DEPART 2.00pm

SYDNEY TO LAUNCESTON THURSDAY 3 MARCH

ANSETT AIRLINES DEPART 10.30

pm

HOBART TO MELBOURNE MONDAY 7 MARCH

ANSETT AIRLINES DEPART 8

/54

5.00pm

93

MELBOURNE TO CANBERRA SATURDAY 12 MARCH

ANSETT

DEPART

E 1.00pm

CANBERRA TO ROCKHAMPTON MONDAY 14 MARCH

ANSETT DEPART

HT 21/89

VE 4.35pm

ANSETT AIRLINES FLIGHT

ANSE

DEPAR

2.00pm

DEF

PERTH TO ADELAIDE DEPART

THURSDAY 18 FEBRUARY ANSETT AIRLINES

pm 54

00pm ADELAIDE TO BRISBANE DEPART 9.45am

WEDNESDAY 24 FEBRUARY DEPART 7.00a

93 COOLANGATTA TO SYDNEY ANSETT AIRLIN

1.00pm ANSETT AIRL

21/89 SYDNEY TO LAUNCESTON DEPART 8.2

4.35pm THURSDAY 3 MARCH QANTAS AI

HOBART TO MELBOURNE DEPART

T 20 MO 7 MARCH CANBERRA DEPART

IV 11.35am ME PTON ANSETT

IGHT 201 S DEPART

RRIVE 9.35am NSVILL ANSE

FLIGHT 354/12/52 CH DEPA

ARRIVE 1.40pm ARWIN

S FLIGHT CH

n ARRIVE DON

NES FLIGHT ARCH

5pm ARRIVE MONDAY 2 ARCH

LINES FLIGHT ANSETT AIRLINES FLIGHT

ARRIV DEPART 10.30am ARRIVE

Autographs later, chaps!

Colour co-ordinated.

NINETEEN

XIX 76 ⇨

CALENDAR

'Can you give us a run-down of an average working day?' is the journalist's stock question, but pretty fruitless as far as Cliff is concerned. The nearest Cliff ever came to discovering a routine was during his theatrical stint in **Time**. For twelve months he revelled in regular hours and daily commuting. It proved a kind of luxury and too short-lived. The 'one day at a time' approach to living returned with a vengeance and today, if you were to ask Cliff what he will be doing next week, he's unlikely to have a clue.

It needs a peculiar sort of personal stamina and agility to move easily and quickly from one project to another, and to remain coolly in control. Somehow he manages it, with a mental fine-tuning process which at least gives others the impression that he's 100 per cent committed to the job in hand.

In reality, there's no calendar year which divides itself up as neatly as the following, but imagine this schedule mixed together and well shaken, and you'll get some inkling of the Cliff Richard lifestyle cocktail.

January

Media Interviews   *The press are constantly hungry, and a pound for every interview given would be a profitable exchange. Cliff is wary of journalists – and who wouldn't be, after a fair share of misquoting and apparent target practice? But few people would guess, least of all the press. Cliff's a born talker, and there's not a journalist alive who could accuse him of being slow of speech! Generally the press are fair and professional. Unfortunately, it's the exceptions that stick in the memory, and if one more reporter trots out the 'Peter Pan of Pop' line . . .*

Talking to the press is a 'reward' for celebrity status. Sometimes an 'in-depth personal profile' tagged 'Exclusive' can last an hour or two. Most of it will read remarkably like the last 'Exclusive', six months before. Maybe it's Cliff's fault. Too bland, his critics might say. Perhaps, after thirty years, there just aren't any new angles left.

You know where you are with radio and television interviews. What you say comes across just as you said it and, if there's a gaffe, there's only yourself to blame. Cliff enjoys the spontaneity of 'live' interviews and broadcasters jump at the opportunity to have him on air.

February/March

Recording   *Over fifty albums in thirty years is an awesome track record. From the days of Norrie Paramor's lush string sounds in EMI's Abbey Road Studios to today's high-tech computer* wizardry, Cliff's approach to studio recording has been consistently workmanlike. Not for him those hideaway studios on remote paradise islands, or interminable remixing, or last-minute delays to await the 'right mood'. Usually, Cliff's albums are buttoned up within eight weeks and, despite the intense effort involved, comprise the most fulfilling and creative segment of the year.

Never suggest to Cliff that it was better in the 'good old days'. Current technology is stimulating and is there to be harnessed. He may not understand how it works, but he's intent to prove that it does!

April

Television   *Not Cliff's favourite medium. Hanging about is a drag, and in television studios there's an abundance of it. Setting up lighting, determining camera shots, and the apparently inevitable technical hiccups, mean that recording one song can take the best part of a day. And always there's a need for artistic compromise. Television speakers at home just aren't designed to transmit full-blooded rock 'n' roll, and it's well-nigh impossible to convey the magic of a live concert performance on the small screen. But, like it or not, television is massively influential and an appearance on a peak-hour show can help a single leap up the charts. Often the cry is for more Cliff on TV. The voices aren't ignored, but it's an art form to be used sparingly.*

May

Videos and Photo Sessions   *Another of the profession's chores, although given a creative and imaginative director, the video – a necessary adjunct of today's singles promotion – can be an exciting and rewarding experience. Being photographed, however, whether for video or for stills, requires maximum patience and composure. Correct lighting is all-important, and it can take seemingly forever to achieve exactly the right throw of light on precisely the critical spot. But, painstaking though it is, Cliff never underestimates its value. A clever lighting man can contribute much to sustaining a youthful image; a bad one can destroy it overnight! Most cameramen agree that Cliff and the lens have a kind of affinity. In real life, perhaps there's the odd wrinkle and fleck of grey. Maybe, out of respect, the camera seems to ignore them!*

June

Tennis and Books   *If you strung together all the hours that Cliff hits balls over the net on his court at home, or at some tennis club in this country or abroad, it would total an impressive chunk of time. And in June, of course, it's watching Wimbledon. It isn't that he refuses to work during the tournament fortnight, but he usually doesn't! For Cliff, tennis is wholly therapeutic. Physically, it provides a valuable work-out and is the essence of his keep-fit routine. Mentally, it's an escape from being Cliff Richard, with every degree of concentration focused on hitting the ball – not just any old way, but textbook fashion!*

And then there are the books. As an author, Cliff doesn't quite match his recording output, and sales aren't exactly comparable, but his publishers aren't grumbling. In case you're wondering whether Mr Versatile sits and sweats over a typewriter for hours, forget it! He writes the easy way – chatting into a tape-recorder, and letting someone else take the strain.

July

Gospel Concerts   *Capturing headlines as much for his religious convictions as for his pop career, Cliff has never kept his faith under wraps. From his initial Christian commitment in the mid-1960s, he's spoken at countless services, rallies and missions, at churches, colleges, and meeting-places around the world. Whenever there's a gap in the professional schedule, the chances are that it will be plugged by a Christian engagement of some kind. His up-front style and his articulate explanations of Christian doctrines have led one eminent churchman to dub him the country's 'leading Christian ambassador'. And, in a recent newspaper poll, readers voted him Britain's most famous Christian – streets ahead, apparently, of the Archbishop of Canterbury!*

Virtually every year since the late '60s, Cliff has set aside a month to perform a series of charity gospel concerts, raising some half-million pounds for the Christian relief and development organisation, Tear Fund, and dozens of other home-based charities.

August

Holiday *Cliff's annual holiday sees him escaping for two or three weeks to the sunshine, probably at his coastal home on the Algarve in Portugal. No autographs, no telephone, no early morning calls, no pressure. For a short while, it's pure self-indulgence – and few would say he hadn't earned it.*

September

Rehearsal *It is long established that 'Cliff in concert' is among the best value-for-money shows in the business. On stage for over two hours, he might well have thirty songs in the 'set', and each one is performed rather than just sung. What the audience sees and hears on the night doesn't come together from a chat over coffee, and sometimes a month of daily rehearsal is responsible for the high level of technical and musical achievement. Often it's a slog, particularly working out and evolving lighting plots and choreography, but it's a creative challenge which Cliff thrives on more than many top-league artists, who tend to leave the 'ideas department' to others.*

October–December

On Tour *For at least three months of every year, Cliff is on the road in the UK or overseas. Physically, it's the most exacting aspect of his career, but by now he's learned to pace himself. Four or five days 'on', two or three 'off', gives the vocal chords opportunity to relax and recover from the pounding of consecutive* concerts. On those 'free' days, it's as though the body knows it's due for a wind-down, and overnight it declines into 'clapped-out mode'. Happily, it's equally sensitive in reverse!

Christmas is invariably at home with the family.

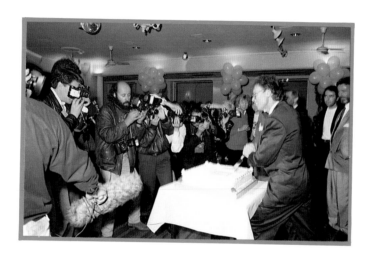

Another batch of questions, opinions and
flashbacks. The ground is familiar, and Cliff
enjoys the cut-and-thrust of spontaneous
interview. He always declines the option of
knowing the questions beforehand.

Sharing recording studios with Aswad.

I could have sworn it went under!

Never too young – or too old! Tennis drills
at Bisham Abbey.

Cliff's input to encourage junior tennis
has given him great pleasure and enabled
hundreds of youngsters to pick up the game.

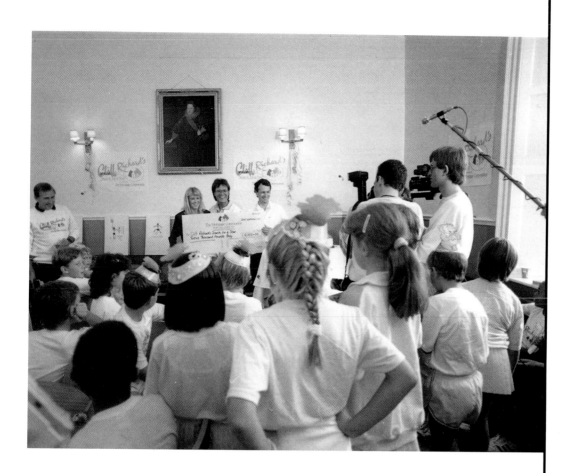

On stage with guests Bruce Welch, Aswad, and Climie Fisher, in aid of The Great Ormond Street Children's Hospital Appeal. Over £120,000 was raised from an evening at the Hammersmith Odeon.

At the beginning it's all very basic.

NINETEEN

XIX 82 ⟳

FAITH

You can be irritated by it, offended, comforted or inspired – but don't doubt the integrity of Cliff's Christian faith. Understandably, there were cynical voices after his first major public reference to his conversion from a Billy Graham platform in the mid-1960s. 'Publicity to support a flagging career,' they said. 'Give it a few months and watch it wear off.' With hindsight, the doubters were proved slightly absurd.

For twenty-five years, Cliff's Christian witness has been forthright and consistent, despite the continuing probe of the media, and his reputation and status as a man of faith now seem inextricably woven with the man of music. Labels such as Britain's 'greatest Christian ambassador' and 'best-known Christian' aren't because of aggressive Bible-bashing. 'I talk about my faith because people ask me,' says Cliff. And when they do, which is certainly often, he gladly jumps in with both feet.

Whatever Cliff puts his mind to, it seems – whether career, tennis or beliefs – he's the ultimate enthusiast. No half measures, everything one hundred and ten per cent! And few would deny that, for Cliff, his life, personality and horizons have been stretched and enhanced by the spiritual dimension. Not for him the negative, restrictive lifestyle of 'thou shalt nots' . . . His association with the relief and development agency Tear Fund, for example, has led him to refugee camps in Bangladesh, to remote bush villages in Southern Sudan, to hospitals in Haiti, and to Mother Teresa's Home for the Destitute and Dying in Calcutta. His willingness to be quizzed about his beliefs and attitudes has taken him to colleges, universities and churches around the world, and his articulate, jargon-free defence and explanation of Christian doctrines have challenged many to enquire further into Christian claims. Cliff's books also – such as You, Me and Jesus *and* Mine To Share *– have instructed and encouraged. Yet in all these things Cliff would claim that he invariably gains, in terms of understanding and confidence, far more than he ever gives out.*

The rock 'n' roll world regards Cliff as an enigma. They respect him immensely and applaud his achievements, but he doesn't fit the earthy mould of 'drugs, sex and rock 'n' roll'. And, for some, that's faintly discomfiting.

Even at gospel events, the media are never far away. At the Greenbelt Christian Festival – one of the country's largest annual open-air music and arts events – Cliff spends much of his time before the performance talking with radio, press and television people. If he sometimes gets fed up to the teeth with it, few would guess.

Maybe Cliff's earned the right to share his
Christian opinions. Certainly his communication
style attracts many listeners.

All Souls Church, next to Broadcasting House
in London, is the venue for the Arts Centre
Group Christmas Celebration. As the wise men
brought their gifts, so the artists offer their
talents.

Discography – Singles

(1)	DB 4178	Move It/Schoolboy Crush	Aug 1958
(2)	DB 4203	High Class Baby/My Feet Hit The Ground	Nov 1958
(3)	DB 4249	Livin' Lovin' Doll/Steady With You	Jan 1959
(4)	DB 4290	Mean Streak/Never Mind	Apr 1959
(5)	DB 4306	Living Doll/Apron Strings	Jul 1959
(6)	DB 4351	Travellin' Light/Dynamite	Oct 1959
(7)	DB 4398	A Voice in the Wilderness/Don't Be Mad At Me	Jan 1960
(8)	DB 4431	Fall In love With You/Willie and the Hand Jive	Mar 1960
(9)	DB 4479	Please Don't Tease/Where Is My Heart?	June 1960
(10)	DB 4506	Nine Times Out of Ten/Thinking of Our Love	Sep 1960
(11)	DB 4547	I Love You/'D' In Love	Nov 1960
(12)	DB 4593	Theme For a Dream/Mumblin' Mosie	Feb 1961
(13)	DC 756	Gee Whiz Its You/I Cannot Find A True Love	Mar 1961
(14)	DB 4667	A Girl Like You/Now's the Time To Fall In Love	Jun 1961
(15)	DB 4716	When The Girl In Your Arms Is The Girl In Your Heart/Got A Funny Feeling	Oct 1961
(16)	DB 4761	The Young Ones/We Say Yeah	Jan 1962
(17)	DB 4828	I'm Looking Out The Window/Do You Want To Dance	May 1962
(18)	DB 4886	It'll Be Me/Since I Lost You	Aug 1962
(19)	DB 4950	The Next Time/Bachelor Boy	Nov 1962
(20)	DB 4977	Summer Holiday/Dancing Shoes	Feb 1963
(21)	DB 7034	Lucky Lips/I Wonder	May 1963
(22)	DB 7089	It's All In The Game/Your Eyes Tell On You	Aug 1963
(23)	DB 7150	Don't Talk To Him/Say You're Mine	Nov 1963
(24)	DB 7203	I'm The Lonely One/Watch What You Do With My Baby	Jan 1964
(25)	DB 7272	Constantly/True True Lovin'	Apr 1964
(26)	DB 7305	On The Beach/A Matter of Moments	Jun 1964
(27)	DB 7372	The Twelfth of Never/I'm Afraid To Go Home	Oct 1964
(28)	DB 7420	I Could Easily Fall (In Love With You)/I'm In Love With You	Dec 1964
(29)	DB 7496	The Minute You're Gone/Just Another Guy	Mar 1965
(30)	DC 762	Angel/Razzle Dazzle	May 1965
(31)	DB 7596	On My Word/Just A Little Bit Too Late	Jun 1965
(32)	DB 7660	The Time In Between/Look Before You Love	Aug 1965
(33)	DB 7660	Wind Me Up (Let Me Go)/The Night	Oct 1965
(34)	DB 7866	Blue Turns To Grey/Somebody Loses	Mar 1966
(35)	DB 7968	Visions/What Would I Do (For The Love Of A Girl)	Jul 1966
(36)	DB 8017	Time Drags By/The La La La Song	Oct 1966
(37)	DB 8094	In The Country/Finders Keepers	Dec 1966
(38)	DB 8150	It's All Over/Why Wasn't I Born Rich?	Mar 1967
(39)	DB 8210	I'll Come Running/I Got The Feelin'	Jun 1967
(40)	DB 8245	The Day I Met Marie/Our Story Book	Aug 1967
(41)	DB 8293	All My Love/Sweet Little Jesus Boy	Nov 1967

(82)	EMI 5251	Daddy's Home/Shakin' All Over	Nov 1981
(83)	EMI 5318	The Only Way Out/Under The Influence	Jul 1982
(84)	EMI 5341	Where Do We Go From Here?/Discovering	Sep 1982
(85)	EMI 5348	Little Town/Love And A Helping Hand/You, Me and Jesus	Nov 1982
(86)	EMI 5385	True Love Ways/Galadriel (both with London Symphony Orchestra)	Apr 1983
(87)	EMI 5415	Never Say Die (Give A Little Bit More)/Lucille	Aug 1983
(88)	EMI 5437	Please Don't Fall In Love/Too Close To Heaven	Nov 1983
(89)	EMI 5457	Baby You're Dynamite/Ocean Deep	Mar 1984
(90)	RICH 1	Shooting From The Heart/Small World	Oct 1984
(91)	RICH 2	Heart User/I Will Follow You	Jan 1985
(92)	EMI 5531	She's So Beautiful/She's So Beautiful (inst)	Sep 1985
(93)	EMI 5537	It's In Every One of Us/Alone (inst)	Nov 1985
(94)	EMI 5544	Born To Rock 'n' Roll/Law Of The Universe (inst)	May 1986
(95)	EM 4	My Pretty One/Love Ya	Jun 1987
(96)	EM 18	Some People/One Time Lover Man	Aug 1987
(97)	EM 31	Remember Me/Another Christmas Day	Oct 1987
(98)	EM 42	Two Hearts/Yesterday, Today, Forever	Feb 1988
(99)	EM 78	Mistletoe & Wine/Marmaduke	Nov 1988
(100)	EM 92	The Best Of Me/Move It	May 1989

Discography – *Albums*

(1)	CLIFF	Apr 1959
(2)	CLIFF SINGS	Nov 1959
(3)	ME AND MY SHADOW	Oct 1960
(4)	LISTEN TO CLIFF	May 1961
(5)	21 TODAY	Oct 1961
(6)	THE YOUNG ONES	Dec 1961
(7)	32 MINUTES AND 27 SECONDS WITH CLIFF RICHARD	Oct 1962
(8)	SUMMER HOLIDAY	Jan 1963
(9)	CLIFF'S HIT ALBUM	Jul 1963
(10)	WHEN IN SPAIN	Sep 1963
(11)	WONDERFUL LIFE	Jul 1964